Conventional Wisdom

By Brian J. McAfee

ISBN 978-0-578-56100-4

Published by Kourindou Books. Georgia, USA.
www.kourindou.us

Author is not responsible for the content of videos linked to in this book. Videos linked in this text may contain adult language or other content not suitable for young viewers. Viewer discretion is advised.

Special thanks to my beta reader Sabrina Makela Davis and my editor Seth (Stephanie) Blackburn for helping me to (hopefully) not sound like an idiot.

Cover: Youtuber Yumi King stands on stage for the opening ceremony at Tiger Con, Valdosta Georgia, 2018. Photo by Erick Requadt.

Contents

Introduction

The Other Side of the Table

I first became an anime fan in the 1980s, long before there was a significant anime industry in the United States. Back before there were anime conventions. Actually, only a few fandoms even had conventions back in those days, and the ones that did exist were much smaller than what we have today. Being an avid fan with a natural tendency to organize events, I started and ran many a fan club in the 80s and 90s, and I even run one today. I always had dreams of leveraging the manpower and enthusiasm of one of those clubs to start a convention. In 2014, I suddenly decided that it was time to make that happen.

That year I was at Con Jikan, an anime convention held at the University of New Mexico in Albuquerque. I had attended at least a dozen cons before that one, but this one felt different. I was over 40, and I had the distinct feeling of being the oldest person at the con. It probably didn't help that nearly all the attendees and staff were college students, but still it felt a bit strange. I felt as if I should be doing something more than just attending. After all, I had been an active member of this fandom for decades, knew lots of members of the anime industry, and because of my 20 years in the military, I knew I had the leadership and management skills to pull it off. It was on that day I decided to make the transition, as I like to put it, to the other side of the table.

What I mean by that is, the average convention attendee is on one side of the table and the people they came to see are on the other. The table I'm referring to is the table at the front of the panel room behind which the panelist or celebrity guest sits, or the table in the dealer's hall or artist alley behind which the artists or vendors sit, or even the registration or information table behind which the staff sits. I wanted to make the transition from the front of the table, where everybody else was, to the back where the people who make it all happen sit.

First, I started as an exhibitor. I have a love of writing, so I began to sell my books at conventions. Then I started hosting panels. This gave me some experience on that other side of the table, and I got to know how vendors, panelists, and exhibitors want to be treated and what pitfalls I could avoid when I started planning these types of events. I got to know some people who ran the conventions, and eventually I weaseled my way into running one. That convention was actually a great first one to be chairman of, since we were partnered with another already successful con. I got to manage the ticket sales, programming, and guest relations side of the con, but the dealer's room and venue were managed by our partner. I'd have to say it was the perfect way to get some experience without having to get in over my head.

The age part of this equation is a variable you may or may not have in common with me, but it was just a catalyst. Your catalyst may be something completely different. In my case, I just felt that at my age, with all my experience and talent, I really should be doing more. I felt a responsibility to contribute to the fandom community in a more meaningful way. By hosting panels, and eventually entire conventions, I was making the community better and more enjoyable for the next generation of fans. I assume that if you're reading this book, for whatever reason, you've felt that same call to give back to your fandom community. I wish you the best of luck. Hopefully this book will guide you in the right direction. At the very least, I hope it helps you avoid some common problems.

The first thing you need to know is that running a convention is not something you should be considering simply because you enjoy anime, comics, cosplay, gaming, etc. Neither should you be considering it because of your love of going to conventions. You should only be considering running a convention if you love leading people and managing resources. It helps a little that you know about the subject matter, but really this will only be a nightmare for you if you aren't already good at leading and managing. Starting a convention is a big job. So, if you already have a real job, and the idea of taking on a second one doesn't appeal to you, then this probably isn't for you. Especially if you aren't willing to be both owner and manager of that second job, because you will be responsible, even financially, if the thing fails.

Despite what many people selling leadership training might tell you, you can't simply study your way to being a good leader. You can get better at it by honing your skills through training, but you have to start with at least some small measure of leadership ability to begin with. It's a part of your personality, like a sense of humor or compassion. Some people, when they are in a group, naturally gravitate toward, or in some cases are thrust into, a position of leadership, and they excel or even enjoy it. These are the natural leaders. The ability to focus on details, make plans and stick with them, keep track of money and put all the pieces of the puzzle together without losing any are necessary traits. These are the skills of a manager. One thing that did stick with me from the volumes of leadership training the Air Force made me take was this: Leaders lead people and managers manage resources. Don't get them confused, because if you try to manage people, it will always be a chore for both you and those under you. And of course, you can't lead resources. Dwight D. Eisenhower said, "Leadership is the art of getting someone else to do something you want done because he wants to do it." That's a perfect description of the kind of person who should run a convention. You don't just tell people what needs to be done and make sure they do it. You share your vision with them and get them to want to achieve it as much as you do. Then all you have to do is guide them. Many hands make light work, and many eager and well led hands can turn work into fun. So, if you're that kind of person then I'll give you some pointers on how to start a convention.

This book is not for the veteran convention organizer. I'm afraid I'll have little to offer you that you haven't already discovered. This book is for the club which wants to start up a first-year convention. It's for someone who may have volunteered, or even staffed a con before, but has never built one from the ground up. I'm not going to tell you how to run Anime Expo or San Diego Comic Con. What I will tell you is how to start up a con which will have two to six guests and perhaps several hundred attendees. Nearly every con starts out here. Momocon, now boasting attendance of over 30,000, started their first year with only 700. This is where you begin, and once you have mastered the basics you can hopefully grow into something bigger.

How do I know what I'm talking about? Because I've done it myself. Not only have I been a panelist and exhibitor at dozens of cons, I also personally know many of the bigger names in the anime industry, so I've heard their horror stories about bad con experiences. And most importantly, I have started two cons from scratch. I started Protoculture Con, the convention celebrating the 30th Anniversary of the animated series Robotech. It was held at the Pasadena Convention Center in Pasadena CA, and we had 10 guests including voice actors, writers, directors, and industry executives. I was brought back to run Protoculture Con for the 35th Anniversary as well. I was able to chair that west coast convention all the way from my home in Georgia, only flying out to California the day before the con. All the work I did leading up to the event made it go smoothly once I got there. I also started Tiger Con, which is a convention first conceived of by the Moody Air Force Base Comics and Anime Club. In our first year we had six guests including a prominent voice actor, a comic book artist, a Youtuber, and three professional cosplayers. Our attendance was approximately 400. The second year for Tiger Con was even better, adding a second voice actor to the guest lineup and attracting approximately 600 attendees. I know that may sound small, since many conventions have attendance in the thousands, but for a small town in South Georgia, that's way better than anyone expected.

That's what I enjoy doing. When people I know say, "I'd like to start a con," I get excited. Sure, I love anime, cosplay, etc., but I also love leading and managing. I love making the big decisions, finding the solutions, and getting people excited about doing tedious, meticulous work. But mostly I love the feeling when it's all done, and I know that I created something that made hundreds of people happy. It can be one of the most rewarding things you will ever do.

In the Air Force we love to follow checklists. It helps you get a complex task done without missing any important steps. You can take someone who is pretty much unfamiliar with the task, give them a checklist, and as long as they have the necessary basic competency, they can complete the job. That's what I have tried to create with this book. It's laid out chronologically for the most part. Start at the beginning and follow it through to the end. You may want to add to what is presented here, and that's great, but I would advise against omitting any part of it. These are the basics, and missing any bit of it could cause you trouble. It won't guarantee your success, but it will help you to avoid failure. Ultimately, it won't make you a convention organizer, but if you are already an organizer, it will give you the convention part. Good luck!

Priorities

I have four priorities when it comes to running a convention, and focusing on those things has worked well for me. Some other cons follow this pattern as well, while some are obviously of a different attitude. Those priorities are: Guests, attendees, staff, and money. In that order. Here's why…

Guests come first. Even before attendees and staff. You invited them. You are using them to bring in the attendees. You need to treat them right, if for no other reason than because it will save you money in the long run. Perhaps I put this one first because I have lived the majority of my life in the southeastern US, where hospitality is a strong tradition.

I have had nearly every anime industry member I know tell me how much they hate a certain major anime convention because they get treated like cattle. They are herded from one event to the next and not given any consideration as a person at all. They hate going to that particular convention, but they keep going year after year. Why? Because they pay well. On the other hand, many of the same people have told me that they prefer smaller conventions, even those which cannot pay much. The reason is that smaller cons treat their guests like people. The guests like interacting with the fans. They like being treated like human beings. In the end, a guest is an investment, but a happy guest who had a fantastic time may ask to come back to your con, and they may be willing to cut you a deal in order to do that.

Next are the attendees. I lump the exhibitors into this category as well. They are the ones ultimately paying the bills so you can have a convention. Make sure you plan everything from their perspective. Everything from the schedule to the traffic flow. Think of how you would want it to work if you had to pay to be there; to wait in the lines and shop in the artist alley and dealer's room. Design everything so that it is easy, simple, and fun. Look at the layout of your dealer's room to make sure people flow in, around, and out in an orderly manner. Make sure you have a good program guide with a schedule, and most importantly, a good map. Have a panel on the last day of your con where attendees can come and tell you how you did. Let them complain about things, or tell you what they would like to be improved at the next con. That's how you get better. Don't argue, just take notes and change what you can. Some things are beyond your control, but listening makes the attendees feel valued. This is a community after all.

Third is the staff. They are going to be the oil that makes your machine run. You need to make them feel important, so they will want to do a good job. Running a convention isn't easy, but many hands make light work. Staff members like exclusive swag. Shirts or fancy badges are a must. They need something they can keep as a memento of the time and effort they put in. You should try to arrange some face time with the guests as a reward for the staff. Providing lunch in the form of a sandwich tray or other inexpensive food is good too. Many will not have time to leave the convention to eat, so setting up a room where they can drop in to grab a drink, a sandwich, or a chicken tender is a must.

Finally is the money. You might think this should be the first thing, and many conventions do. However, if you put the money first, you may be tempted to overlook some of the other things I have listed here. The budget is the boundary inside which you must operate when taking care of the other priorities. You should expect to probably lose money on your first year, but if you took care of your guests, attendees, and staff, then next year will be better, and likely profitable. Having guests, attendees, and staff who want to come back next year is a recipe for success. Losing any one of those is a recipe for disaster. Still, the bottom line is the bottom line. You can't do everything you want to do in your first year, and you are going to have to decide if certain things fit into your budget or if they will just have to wait for next year. A prime example is the decision to have a rave or not. Lots of people will get excited if you advertise that you will have a rave at your convention, and yes, that does translate into extra ticket sales. Also, surprisingly, it isn't difficult to contract a vocaloid concert for your con. However, a rave means hiring a DJ, extra insurance, and possibly extra security. You may need to keep your venue open later, increasing the cost of the location. Vocaloids need equipment and crew which have to be transported across the country or even internationally. You have to decide if these extra costs are worth the extra ticket sales. For most young conventions, it isn't.

The Vision

The first step is the vision. Someone must have a picture in their head of just what they want to do. You also need to be able to communicate that vision, because the second thing you need is a team. I suppose you could say the third thing you need is time, and by that I mean if you think you are going to have a convention next month you're a fool. Give yourself a year to plan and prepare.

There isn't much to say about the vision. It pretty much only includes the most basic details such as what type of convention you want to hold, what type of events you want to include, and what town to hold it in; and I advise you to pick your own town. Traveling to another town to hold the con only multiplies your work load, as I know from experience. Even if a neighboring town has better facilities, it will also add extra problems.

The vision helps you to focus. Will it be an anime con, comic con, or something else? You may be tempted to do an all-inclusive fandom con, and those are certainly popular. This is entirely up to you, but I will give you one piece of advice. The tighter your focus, the smaller your budget. If, for example, you want to do comics, gaming, cosplay and anime, then you will feel pressured to have guests from each category. Now you are expected to have a comic book artist, gamer or game designer, professional cosplayer, and a voice actor at your con. Maybe you should just stick with one for your first year. The flip side of that coin is that the more fandoms you appeal to, the more people will come to your con. More people at the con means more tickets sold, and more money to work with. However, I still advise starting small and working up.

The next step is to assemble a team. At first you don't need a big one, but you need the ability to recruit 10 to 20 before the doors open. Assuming you are the chairperson, you should start out with a treasurer and a public relations officer. That's because you will need these officers before any others. You can add the rest later.

The treasurer must be a part of the con from day one. You need someone to keep you on track so you don't overspend. One thing you will find out quickly is that everyone has great ideas that they want to implement, but you probably don't have the money to do most of them. You also need detailed records of how the money was raised and how it was spent. There are ways to attain tax free status for your club or your convention. Many cons do this, but many don't. Either way, you may need to show records to the government to justify your tax situation, and of course, you will also be accountable to the rest of your team to assure them the money is being handled responsibly. That's why the treasurer should be the first officer you recruit.

Second is the public relations officer. You need to get the word out. Social media is great, but you need more than that. You need to be setting up tables at other conventions and advertising for your con. You need to find out what clubs meet in your area and where you can tell fans that you are starting a convention for them. You need local businesses to put up flyers for you. And, most importantly, you need to attract sponsors. You may subdivide the office later, with one officer responsible for your online presence, one solely responsible for sponsors, etc., but at first, this will likely all fall to your public affairs person. Get them involved early.

Up to this point, it's been simple. Now you arrive at the first hurdle. You require three basic elements in order to have a convention. If you are missing any one of these three, you don't have anything but a dream. They are: a name, a venue, and a date. Sounds easy, but it's really not. Finding a catchy name that isn't already taken is difficult, and you should do online searches and check sites such as animecons.com or fancons.com to make sure you aren't hijacking someone else's great name. Look back years into the records because you also don't want to pick the name of a con that failed since people might associate you with that con if you use the same name. Second, you can't just pick a date. You can have a preference, but until you find a venue there can be no date. This will take a while. You need to select a few locations that would serve your purposes and then go check them out in person. Something that looks great online may have fatal flaws like narrow hallways or something you never thought of until you saw it for yourself. Once you narrow it down to a few good candidates, you compare prices. Finally, you see if they are available on the date you want. You can't advertise or invite guests until you have a location and date locked in. Once you find a venue that is suitable for your event and available on the date you want, that's when the real problem begins: money.

Money

If you have dreams of getting rich running a convention, let me tell you that's probably not realistic. Actually, while a lot of money does change hands as part of a convention (Anime Expo has a budget of over $3M), that doesn't translate into people getting paid a lot. If you are somehow able to grow your convention into one that attracts thousands of attendees, you may be able to get some kind of compensation for the work you put into it, but this is not a path to fame and riches. For one thing, conventions tend to grow and require more money each year than the last. What you make this year will almost certainly have to be rolled into next year. So where does the money for year one come from?

It's the chicken or the egg paradox. You can't get a venue and date until you get some money, but you can't raise any money until you have a venue and date. Most venues won't let you reserve a date without a deposit, and in many cases, that can be as much as half the total cost of the venue. It can be as much as a few thousand dollars up front to reserve a good venue. So where do you get the money for that? Doing a fundraiser for a convention without a date and venue won't work. Nobody is going to donate to that. Of course, having a big name associated with the con would help raise money, but I don't care if you personally know a voice actor, comic book artist, or other celebrity, they aren't going to commit to a con without a solid date. I also doubt a sponsor would chip in anything until you get those two magic ingredients of venue and date. So how do you get past this first hurdle? Gambling.

No, I don't mean put it all on black and hope for the best. I mean you are probably going to have to risk some of your own money. If you have a club, you can raise the money through various fundraisers, but club fundraisers usually raise hundreds of dollars, not thousands. If you legally register your club with the IRS and get an Employee Identification Number, you can get credit and open a bank account for your club. But in the end, you are most likely going to have to risk some of your own money, and success is definitely not assured. You are putting money down on a dream.

There are ways to limit the risk. Like I stated earlier, you can get a credit card for your club. If you find a venue that will give a full refund if you cancel, then you won't be stuck paying off a credit card if you aren't able to pull the convention off. To be honest, the venue and some advertising is all you will likely have to pay for up front. The financial landscape at the time of writing this book is such that many credit card companies are offering cards with zero interest for twelve or even fourteen months. That means as long as your convention breaks even, you can pay off the card and never pay any interest. It requires solid budgeting and realistic estimates of the number of tickets you are likely to sell, but it can be done. Tiger Con is always funded in this way.

Once you have the two magic ingredients of venue and date, you can raise money through various means. Crowdfunding and promotional items are two options.

Crowdfunding

There are several crowdfunding platforms out there, and they each have their pros and cons. For instance, let's compare Kickstarter and Go Fund Me. Go Fund Me lets you keep whatever money is pledged whether or not you meet your goal. Kickstarter is all or nothing. If you don't reach your goal, no money changes hands. At first, Go Fund Me sounds like the way to go, but consider this. If your goal is $5000 but you only raise $1000, can you still hold the convention? Probably not, especially if you were being honest about needing 5K. But now you have received funds from people who expect rewards and a convention. If you cancel because you didn't raise enough, you are now responsible for paying those investors back. This gets even more complicated if you already spent some of the money before deciding to cancel.

A crowdfunding campaign is also a great way to gauge the interest for a con in your area. If you don't reach your goal, then you probably wouldn't have many people attending your con, so maybe it would be better if no money was exchanged if you missed the funding goal. Consider carefully when choosing your platform.

The first year of Tiger Con used a Kickstarter campaign to raise funds, but we didn't meet our goal. In that case, no money changed hands and we didn't have the problem of repaying investors. Despite our failed campaign, we decided to proceed by using credit to pay for expenses. I bring this up to make sure you understand that crowdfunding for a first-year convention is very difficult. People don't want to risk their money on an unproven concept. Yet they may still come to your con if you are able to pull it off. Actually, despite advertising and offering tickets for the con for nearly a full year, we sold over 90 percent of our tickets in the four weeks leading up to the con. Judging interest is very difficult for a first-year con.

When setting up your crowdfunding campaign, consider three things. First, have several pledge levels so people with varying budgets can participate. A one or five dollar level is a good place to start. For the higher levels, people will want rewards. You can make lots of different incentives. For Tiger

Con we did challenge coins, patches, buttons featuring images of our mascot, VIP tickets to the con, and autographed items signed by the guests of honor. Just keep in mind that the dollar amount of the pledge has to cover the cost of the reward, shipping, and any fees charged by the platform, and still make some money for the con.

The second thing to consider is the goal. You don't need to raise the total cost of the convention. There will still be ticket sales, sponsors, dealer booths and artist alley tables to bring in money. Think of the things you need to pay for up front, before the ticket sales start. The venue is the big one. Advertising is another. For the advertising budget consider the cost of online ad campaigns, website, banners, flyers, and maybe even trips to other cons to advertise your con. Altogether, your goal should probably be the cost of your venue plus about 30 percent. The 30 percent will cover the cost of producing rewards, advertising, and the cut that the crowdfunding platform will take. Another way to set a goal, if you have multiple guests, is to make your goal the total cost of bringing in guests. This can vary considerably due to multiple factors which will be explained later, but it can often be the most expensive part of the convention. Whichever way you go, make sure you do not break the cardinal rule of convention organizing. Never, ever, announce a guest until they have been confirmed.

The third thing to consider is fulfillment. If you have physical rewards, you will have to get them to people. This can be an expensive proposition. You pretty much have two options. You can get a fulfillment company (just google it, there are many) to ship the rewards to your backers, or you can stuff envelopes and address packages yourself. Depending on how much time and manpower you have, the latter might be best. You can add a shipping fee to your pledge levels which have physical rewards, but those shipping costs may count toward your total goal. If your pledge level is $100, and you also charge $10 each to ship the reward to these backers, then Kickstarter will show that you have raised $1100 after ten people have pledged that level, not $1000 which is what you actually raised. This can cause you to prematurely hit your goal before you have actually reached the funding you need. A way to reduce this disparity is to have your backers pick up their rewards along with their badge when they check in at the convention. You may still want to have some rewards that will ship, since not everyone who wants to back your project will make it to the con.

In order to set up a crowdfunding campaign, you will need a bank account. I advise against using a personal account, no matter how much you trust the person whose account it is. Be professional and open an account just for your club, or just for the convention. Keep all the convention money separate from anyone's personal money. In order to open a business account, you will need an Employer Identification Number, which can be obtained online from the IRS by filling out a simple form. It takes minutes. Just keep in mind that you will have to file tax returns for this convention, but don't worry too much; first year conventions rarely make money, so you probably won't owe much, or anything. Keep track of all your expenses.

Promotional Items

You can make money by selling promotional items. There are many ways to do this, but keep in mind a few guiding principles.

First, make them something people will want to have even if the con never happens. For Tiger Con, we made military style challenge coins with our con mascot on them. Lots of people loved the idea of

Tiger Con Challenge Coin (Year Two). Photo by author.

a collectible coin with an anime character on it and were very willing to buy them.

You can also simply use items that people want, such as figurines, comics, manga, etc. I'm not advocating setting up a retail business. You can raffle these items. Tiger Con made hundreds of dollars by offering raffle boxes filled with donated items like these. Businesses are often willing to donate items rather than money, but you can turn those items into funds by raffling them, especially at other cons. Get a fan table at a nearby convention. While you are handing out flyers and talking to people, make sure they know that you are raffling off a box of anime or comic themed goodies for just a dollar per ticket. Maybe even throw a weekend pass to your convention into the basket too. It costs you nothing, and people see extra value in the prize. Just make sure to ask the convention organizer for permission to sell items or raffle tickets. Many cons offer free tables under the expectation that you aren't using them to make money. Still, if you are only raising money to fund your convention, they often agree to let you sell.

The second thing to consider is selling items which serve dual purpose as advertising. Pin back buttons with your mascot on them, T-shirts, etc., are all good ways to raise some money and get the word out about your convention. If you are part of a club, you'll be surprised how many of your members will buy these shirts and other items. Items such as these not only raise money, but people see them and ask about the con. Putting your

Tiger Con Promo Items. Photo by Eric Requadt.

adorable convention mascot on a shirt or button builds interest. If you wear the shirt around town, or at another convention, always have some business cards with your convention information to hand out to anyone who shows interest.

One note of caution on shirts. Because you need several sizes and don't know which sizes are going to be popular, it's easy to get left with a bunch of shirts that didn't sell, which means wasted money. One way to avoid this is to purchase a screen-printing machine and only make shirts as they are needed. You can get a single-color screen printing press for about $300. Alternately, you could do iron on images which have the same benefit of preventing waste. In both cases you are trading your time and effort for the benefit of maximizing your fundraising efficiency. However, if you do decide to have the shirts professionally printed, make sure to order less than you think you can sell. If you think you can sell 200, but only sell 100, then you probably lost money. If you think you can sell 200, but only order 100 yet you sell out your entire stock, then you definitely made money. Better to miss out on some potential than to lose money because you overestimated.

Program Guide

Your convention program guide serves two purposes. It provides information to your attendees so they know what's going on and where. It also serves as a promotional item which makes you money. This fundraising is through the selling of advertising.

A good program guide has certain necessary elements. As a minimum it should have the schedule, a map of the venue, a list of your sponsors, and the guest biographies. You can sell full and half page ads inside the guide, as well as the back cover. Other things you may want to include are your convention policies and rules, a list of your staff, a map of the dealer room showing which dealers are located where, and descriptions of all your events. For a small convention you may be tempted to print the guide yourself, but unless you have a professional quality printer, it's better to just have a printing service produce them.

Once you include the cost of printer ink, paper, and the time you will spend folding and stapling, it just isn't worth it.

I highly advise sending your guide to the printing service with enough time to print it again if it comes back with flaws. One year, I had the printing service lose the order and I didn't have enough time to put the order in again and still have it delivered before the doors opened for the con. That's how I know just how much work and money goes into making them yourself. I stayed up an entire night, along with several of my staff, no sleep, printing, folding, and stapling program guides so we would have enough for the first day. The professionally printed ones came in for the second day, and the company did give me a significant discount, but the damage was done. Learn from my mistake and send the order to the print company about a month before the date of the con. It does put some pressure on your programming director to finish the schedule early, but it's better than having a last-minute problem with the guide.

You should also consider supplementing your program guide with an event app. Two apps which I am familiar with are Fan Guru and Whova. Both will provide you with a top quality service. They allow you to upload your entire schedule, panel and event descriptions, guest bios, etc. This is almost the same as having the program guide right on your phone or other personal electronic device. One significant benefit is that attendees can use the app to coordinate meetups such as photo shoots, or to find out which of their friends will be attending certain events.

Ticketing Service

Attendees like to wait until the last possible minute to buy tickets, so don't count on ticket sales for money early on. However, vendors and other exhibitors like to get a space as early as possible so they don't miss out. Some of the earliest money you will raise will likely be from dealers and artists purchasing tables and booths. While you can invoice your dealers and artists directly, you can also use your ticketing service as a way for exhibitors to pay for their spaces. Because of this you need to set up your ticketing service early on. This should probably be the very next step after setting your date, venue, and creating a website.

There are many online ticketing services out there. Examples include Eventbrite, Ticketleap, and GrowTix. As an exhibitor, I have used GrowTix to pay for my exhibit space at conventions. It seemed to work just fine and it allowed for the purchaser to put in lots of info so the event managers knew exactly who I was and what I was paying for. In my experience, as far as advertising for your event, Eventbrite is better at getting the word out to potential customers. I have received notifications from Eventbrite about many events that they thought would interest me. However, I haven't used them to ticket my events. I have used Ticketleap, and I can say that they offer significant flexibility with a fairly easy to use interface. You can set up multiple types of tickets, discounts, and a customized page for your event. Ticketleap also makes it easy to associate your ticketing site with your social media outlets. Ticketleap does charge a fee which scales with the price of the tickets. However, there is no fee for free tickets, such as children's tickets. The only potentially negative issue is that you will receive the full amount your attendees pay for the ticket, and then Ticketleap will charge your account in order to collect the fees. Effectively the purchaser is paying the fee, but Ticketleap doesn't take the fees out at the time of purchase, but rather charges them to your account in batches, probably based on a standardized schedule. It just seems strange to me and I thought it was important to mention. This can cause trouble if you take money out of your account, and then an unexpected charge from Ticketleap comes in causing an overdraft.

Setting up a second ticket campaign, apart from your attendee tickets, just for your dealers and artists to pay for their booths is advisable. Having the dealer and artist tickets included with the general attendees can cause confusion. Anyone who goes to your ticket site may think they can become a dealer or artist just by purchasing a dealer or artist ticket. However, if you set up a second site just for dealers and artists, you can keep that url secret, and only send it to your approved artists and dealers.

Sponsors

You may be thinking that you will get money from sponsors. Think again. In today's economy nobody wants to give you money. I know you see Funimation, Crunchyroll, and Aniplex logos on other convention's badges and lanyards, but that doesn't mean they gave any money to the con. More than likely they only gave permission to show their titles in the viewing room, or maybe some prizes for the convention's contests. If you actually want money, there are two ways to get it.

Local businesses, especially those who are directly related to the theme of your convention and are likely to benefit from the exposure, may be willing to chip in a bit. Many are keen to supply prizes for your contests. The key is to go speak to them in person and sell the idea of how they are going to benefit. To get actual money from them, you are going to have to sell them something: advertising. Sell them a full or half page advertisement in the program guide. Offer them the back page of the program guide too. If the venue allows it, tell them that for a reasonable donation, they can set up a sign or banner at the convention. Also let them know you are willing to put their logo or business name on your website, social media pages, badges, lanyards, shirts, etc. They may not be willing to simply give out money, but they may be willing to purchase advertising at an event where hundreds of their potential customers will be. Again, you will have better luck with the local businesses since 300 potential customers means a lot more to the comic shop at the mall than it does to Marvel, Disney, or Funimation.

One of the best ways to find sponsors is by looking at the sponsor lists from other, nearby cons. By far the most effective means of attracting sponsors for Tiger Con was by emailing businesses who had sponsored similar conventions. Some bought advertising, and that was a big help. Others provided prizes… so many prizes. The photo I posted online of table after

Some of the prizes donated for the first year of Tiger Con. Photo by author.

table full of prizes surely brought in attendees hoping to take some of them home.

Local businesses are a great source of donated prizes.

While geography does factor into the likelihood of getting a sponsor, in today's electronic marketplace, it isn't as important as you might think. While some businesses are looking to increase foot traffic to their store, others want clicks and visits to their website. You'd be surprised, but a kimono shop in New York may be willing to sponsor your convention in South Georgia if it means their logo and web address get in front of people who are likely to buy their product.

One additional word of caution on money and budgeting. Just because you got the convention center for $3000 doesn't mean it will cost you $3000. There are lots of little hidden fees that will come back to bite you on the day of the event. $200 for chairs, $100 for a sound system and microphone, $65 for a TV or projector, $35 per booth for electricity, etc. You will also get nickel and dimed by the small items you need on the day of the convention. From cord to string up banners, to tape, to markers, and even lunch for your guests and/or staff. Make sure to account for those costs in your budget.

Once the ball gets rolling and tickets start selling, you will have to deal with refund requests. Exhibitors and attendees alike will have things come up which prevent them from attending your event. The benefit of having a refund policy is that people are more likely to pre-register. Pre-registration means more money coming in before the doors open and that is a good thing. Money now is always better than money later. However, a refund policy can make it more difficult for you as the organizer.

In my experience, as an attendee and exhibitor at dozens of conventions, a no refund policy is not uncommon. Especially when attendance is capped at a certain number of tickets, a no refund policy makes sense. If you cap your attendance and actually meet that cap, a refund is just an empty seat because ticket sales have ended. It's not like that ticket goes back into the pool and another customer has a chance to get it. Then again, if you aren't capping attendance, or if you do but don't reach the cap, why not offer a refund?

A good compromise is to offer refunds up until a specific date, such as 30 days before the convention. People who regularly go to conventions will not be surprised that you do not offer last minute refunds, especially since many cons don't offer refunds at all. Vendors and exhibitors should be (but often aren't) even more understanding than regular attendees. It is much harder to replace a vendor at the last minute than it is to replace an attendee. A vendor who cancels with less than a month of notice probably means you will have an empty booth in your exhibit hall or dealer room. For this reason, I would advise at least a 30 day notice policy for vendor refunds, if you offer refunds at all.

One last tip is to make sure you have enough cash. Money from ticket sales and vendors will come in well in advance of the convention. You may be tempted to pay down your debt with this first influx of income, and that is a good idea, but make sure you have enough cash on hand to cover your guest appearance fees. Many guests will specify that they want to be paid in cash, and some will even specify that they will be paid on arrival. If your bank account is empty because you paid all your debt off with it, you won't have enough cash on hand to pay your guests. At-the-door ticket sales will produce a lot of cash, but that doesn't help you if the guest wants to be paid upon arrival, the day before the con.

Venue

So now you've got some money and you're ready to lock in a location. You're probably looking for a place that will have space for your events: A large hall for the dealer room, a big auditorium for the main events, artist alley, meeting rooms for panels, etc. However, these aren't the only considerations to look for in a venue. You should also make sure to consider the following: Is it near a hotel and food? Your guests will need to stay somewhere, and if the con is inside an actual hotel then problem solved. Otherwise you will have to arrange transportation to and from the convention for your guests. Also, you don't want people leaving and not coming back. Make sure there is somewhere either at the con, or within walking distance where they can eat.

If you go with a hotel, then ask them for a discount on the convention space if you also book rooms and food. Most hotels will work with you on this. You are going to have to book rooms for your guests anyway, so maybe that will count toward earning a discount. Just be careful of guaranteeing a block of rooms for your attendees. Arranging for a group rate is something you should definitely do, and the hotel will almost certainly give you a group discount code or specific booking URL for your attendees to use, but they may want you to pay for any rooms that don't get filled. This is called attrition. For instance, if you guarantee the hotel that they will rent 100 rooms to attendees, but they only rent 75, then you may have to pay for the other 25. Fortunately, many hotels are willing to negotiate, but I advise going with the smallest number of rooms you need in order to get the discount. Try to avoid an attrition clause completely if at all possible. One way to avoid an attrition clause is to only have the discount for a limited period. For Tiger Con, we offered a group rate so long as you booked your room more than 30 days before the convention. That way, the hotel was able to sell the rooms in our group block to other customers if they didn't get filled with attendees. Actually, we filled the block of rooms and had to increase the number of rooms in our block, which made the hotel very happy and they ended up extending the deadline for people to use the group rate. But the initial group rate deadline of 30 days did reassure the hotel up front and allow us to avoid an attrition clause.

One trick that has worked extremely well for Tiger Con is to work food into the deal. Hotels and convention centers with banquet or restaurant facilities make money from selling food. The food and beverage director may be willing to work with you to reduce the overall price of the venue if food sales are included. There are a couple of ways you can do this. One is to schedule a "VIP dinner" for attendees who purchase a special ticket. You sell twenty or forty of these VIP tickets and price them high enough to cover the cost of dinner. Reserve the hotel restaurant or convention center banquet room for dinner where your VIP attendees can have a meal with the guests of honor. I have done this at least three times and it has been a fantastic success every time. The restaurant/hotel makes money on the food sales and the VIP attendees get a truly unique opportunity to interact with their favorite guest. Just make sure not to oversell this. A good rule of thumb is no more than 10 VIP tickets per guest of honor. Any more than that and you risk the VIP ticket holders feeling like they are lost in the crowd. You want the ratio of attendees to guests to be low so they get some one-on-one conversation with the guests. That's what they paid for after all.

Another way to turn food sales into income is through a maid café. The maid café is a staple of anime conventions, but most are fairly amateur. The average maid café in an American anime convention consists of a group of volunteers dressed as maids, and occasionally butlers, offering light fare such as pastries, cakes, or sandwiches along with entertainment in the form of an act or dance, or just outstanding customer service with kawaii (cute) elements to make the customer feel special. The food is almost always prepared by the maids and is only satisfying if you consider that you are really there for the entertainment, not a meal. However, most convention venues have a kitchen or restaurant. If you can convince the venue to have their kitchen or restaurant prepare the food for the maid café, you can offer professionally prepared meals to the maid café patrons. The proceeds from the sale of the food can go to the convention center, which can be credited toward the cost of the venue, thereby reducing the amount you, as the convention organizer, have to pay. The maids can keep the tips they receive, the hotel/convention center keeps the money from food sales, and you get a discount on the price of the venue. Everybody wins.

Be careful not to book too much venue for your needs. First year conventions tend to have attendance numbers in the hundreds, not the thousands. For an example of what not to do, see Dashcon. (https://www.youtube.com/watch?v=1ZgxeX2dCnQ) There is no shortage of suitable convention venues available in the Chicago area. Despite this, Dashcon booked a large venue capable of handling a crowd of 5,000 for their first year. Video from the convention indicates that less than 1,000 showed up. Some estimates put attendance at under 500. Panelists, guests, and entertainers either cancelled without notice, or the convention organizers knew ahead of time about the cancellations, but neglected to tell the attendees until the day of the con. They changed their refund policy on the day of the con, so that they didn't have to give people back their money.

The biggest lesson to take from Dashcon is that it's better to underestimate attendance than to overestimate. If you book a venue that's too small, you may be left with some regrets that you didn't reach your full potential. If you book a venue that's too big, you will probably be left with a large debt.

Another first year convention had the opposite problem. Tanacon (https://www.youtube.com/watch?v=wDUoDbXvC8o) booked a small venue, but had a massive turnout on the order of thousands more people than they could fit in the venue. It was a disaster with thousands of people standing in line outside the building getting dehydrated and sunburnt. The organizers actually planned it this way, believing this would be good for ticket sales because nothing attracts a crowd like a crowd, but it was actually a recipe for a lawsuit. Whatever size venue you book, find out the maximum capacity and cap ticket sales at that level. That way when you reach your cap, you can tell people so they don't stand in line all day long in vain. It also keeps you out of trouble when it comes to fire codes.

Don't let your venue convince you that you need pipe and drape walls in the dealer room. Some conventions do separate each booth with pipe and drape, but many don't. I have spoken to dealers who would rather not have it. It can get in the way of their setup and just cause problems. It does look professional, and defines each dealer's space, but it isn't essential. One dealer told me he would rather just have his space identified by tape on the floor than pipe and drape. This can be a way to save hundreds of dollars on venue cost.

So now you have the three magical ingredients: a name, a venue, and a date. Congratulations, you have the foundation for a convention, now it's time to start building. This is the time to do two things. First, the aforementioned fundraising, and the second is inviting guests.

Guests

When dealing with celebrity guests, there are three cardinal rules which you should NEVER break. To do so may get you blacklisted with other guests in the industry and make it nearly impossible to get guests for your con in the future. These three rules are very simple. First, never announce a guest until you have confirmed them. In some cases, this is just an agreement made in email or other correspondence, in others it is a full contract, but don't confuse interest with confirmation. Confirmation means you have worked out all the details and an agreement has been reached and finalized.

The second rule is to never publicly reveal the terms of the guest's appearance (fees, conditions, special requests, etc).

Don't tell other convention organizers, other guests, or really anyone who doesn't have a need to know what the guests were offered in exchange for their appearance. One guest finding out what another was offered may feel slighted. If a guest has given you a great deal on their appearance, letting other convention organizers know may undermine that guest when they negotiate for future appearances. Just don't do it.

And finally, never announce that a guest has turned you down. I'm not talking about a guest who has an agreement with you and then has to cancel. Of course you should announce that. People are expecting to see the guest and will feel cheated if they arrive at the convention to find that the guest isn't there. Let people know as soon as possible if a guest who was publicly announced will not be able to make it. But never tell anyone that you tried to get a certain guest and they said no. Guests don't want fans to know that they turned down an appearance. If for some reason you weren't able to come to an agreement, it's best that the public never knew that the guest was ever under consideration. The last thing you want is for fans to find out that a guest has turned down an appearance at your con, causing the fans to start a campaign of pleading with the guest to show up. Now the guest is under pressure to appear at your con or risk disappointing their fans or, in the worst cases, they could face fan backlash, and you don't want to be the cause of that. Word will get around pretty quickly among other potential guests to avoid you.

When inviting guests, first ask if you actually know any. Sometimes, even if you aren't "friends" with a celebrity, maybe you have interacted with them at a few conventions in the past. If they might recognize your name or face, then I'd start with them. If there's some recognition there, they may be more likely to work with you when your budget won't cover their usual appearance fee. Another tip is to go directly to the guest, rather than through an agency. Agencies take a cut and raise costs. Some celebrities will insist that you work through their agent, while others are happy to interact directly with you.

If you don't already have their contact information, start by checking their official websites. Many of them have contact info posted just for this reason. If that fails, try social media. Many respond quickly to a Facebook message or other messaging service. Note: I mean a private message. Obviously don't post your invitation where the public can see it. Many actors and artists are also listed on Linkedin and similar sites. Just remember to be professional and courteous. You aren't offering them a job so much as you are asking them to do you a favor. Sure, you will be paying them, but the purpose of having guests at your convention is because their name sells tickets. Never forget that.

Interestingly enough, you don't actually have to actively invite guests. The most popular guests are invitation only, of course. However, just list your convention on Fancons.com or any of the other online convention databases, and within weeks some of the up and coming actors, actresses, DJs, cosplayers, etc., will ask you for an invitation. They want to get their name out there and move up the ladder of popularity, and because of that they probably won't ask for much of an appearance fee. The flip side of that coin is that they probably won't sell many tickets…this year. The benefit of inviting these guests is that they will work for you. By that, I mean they will host panels and do presentations, be "celebrity guest judges" at your contests, etc. Your attendees will get to interact with them in a more personal manner than they would with the big names, and they will enjoy it a lot. So, your attendees may not have bought a ticket because of the relatively new voice actress who you contracted as a guest, but after they have had fun at her events and panels, they will remember it and probably buy a ticket next year, and they may bring their friends too.

Guests are one of the most important parts of your con, and they should be treated as such. You should have a guest relations representative to deal with the guests. This should be someone personable, friendly, and trustworthy. They will be the face of your convention to the guests. You should also, on the day of the convention, have someone individually assigned to escort each guest from event to event and assist them as necessary. They may have to handle money if the guests collect fees for autographs, so again, they must be trustworthy. They will probably be taking the guests to lunch as well. Their job is to make sure the guest is taken care of in every way, within reason.

The best way I have found to save money on guests is to find some that are within driving distance. Fortunately, Tiger Con is located within driving distance of both Atlanta and Orlando. Both locations are home to some fantastic gaming, comic, and anime guests. Protoculture Con is held in Pasadena, California, which is within driving distance of approximately half of the potential guests associated with the US anime industry and most live action movie guests. An airline ticket, especially from the opposite coast, can cost a lot. You can save hundreds of dollars by finding a local celebrity guest. Of course, that's not always possible, but you should at least take travel expenses into consideration when recruiting guests.

Guests often have special requests. Anything from dietary requirements to specific types of rooms they want to stay in. It's best to get that info early so you can plan for it. Some will provide their own transportation to the con while others will expect you to arrange for every detail. When I say every detail, I mean it. They may want you to arrange for an Uber or taxi to take them from their house to the airport, and likewise from the airport to the convention hotel. It's important to get these details early and make sure they are all spelled out in the contract.

Guests may want you to pay for their meals as well. Paying for meals is actually an opportunity for you to make back some of the money you are pouring into the guest. You can provide them with a per-diem with which they can buy their own food, or you can provide their actual meals. If you make one of those provided meals a VIP dinner, you can charge extra for attendees to come to that dinner. Attendees will pay a premium price for dinner with the guest of honor. Make sure the guest knows they are expected to attend such a dinner. Including it in the contract is the best way to do so. Just remember that the price for these VIP tickets must cover the cost of food, any promotional items (swag) you give to the purchaser, plus the cost of a normal ticket.

While not strictly necessary, it is a great idea to have a specific space for the guests to escape the fans between scheduled events. This is often referred to as a green room. Dealing with adoring fans is what most celebrities love to do, but it can be exhausting. Rather than having them eat in the same hotel or convention center restaurant as the regular attendees, having a special room where they can eat without being disturbed is highly recommended. This also gives them a place to hang out after the con as well, especially if you cater. I have seen some conventions provide a bartender to serve drinks to the guests after convention hours, and others which did not. In my experience, if there is alcohol available at the venue, that's where many of the guests will hang out at after hours. Some want to go to the hotel bar and have a drink with fans. Others want time away from fans in order to relax.

High quality guests are an investment. Paying for them is done in one of two ways. Anime conventions, as opposed to comic conventions, typically pay the guests outright for their appearance. This means negotiating a fee that is paid directly to the guest, usually on arrival, and often in cash. The benefit is that the guest does not charge for autographs, and the attendees really like this. However, some guests are too expensive to pay outright, or perhaps you have too many guests to pay for them up front. Comic conventions traditionally allow the guests sell autographs as payment for their appearance. This works well for big conventions with tens of thousands of attendees, but not so well for a small, first year con where the potential number of autographs sold will be limited. Also, when doing the autograph sales method, guests will usually have the convention guarantee a certain amount of revenue. If you guarantee at least $3000 in autograph sales, and the guest only sells $2000, then the convention will be responsible for making up the other $1000. In recent years, the trend is that conventions are becoming more universal, combining anime, sci-fi, and comic elements, and many combine guest payment methods. For that reason, you may see one guest signing autographs for free, while the one right next to them is charging a fee.

Whichever payment scheme you decide to use, set a guest budget. Account for transportation, food, hotel, etc., in that budget and stick to it. Your attendees and even staff will have fantastic suggestions for potential guests. Many guests and their agents will even contact you asking for an invite. You can't invite them all. You must balance how much money you expect that guest will raise for the convention in terms of ticket sales against the cost of getting that guest to your convention and back home again. If the cost of having the guest is modest, and they are well known enough to generate ticket sales, then you should invite them. But keep in mind that you can't invite every guest you want to have at your con. You need to have a set dollar amount to spend on guests so you know when to stop sending invitations.

In the worst situations, some of your staff may approach potential guests to talk about appearing at your convention without your knowledge. If a guest was approached by a staff member and they feel as if they were "officially invited," then it can be an embarrassing situation to un-invite them if you can't afford their appearance. Alternately, if the unauthorized staff member's invitation has obligated you to have that guest at your convention, that may just blow your budget and put your con in financial trouble. Make sure your ENTIRE staff know that they are not authorized to invite guests. You may want to entirely prohibit them from talking to potential guests about appearing at your con. Alternately, you could allow them to gauge a guest's interest, but ensure that if they do speak to a guest about the con, they must explicitly state that they do not have the authority to extend an official invitation.

Another lesson I learned the hard way is that not all guests get along with each other. Some have personal or professional differences with other members of the industry. Some may simply request not to be scheduled to be on a panel with certain other guests, while others may cancel their entire appearance if they learn that a certain person is also a guest. For this reason, you should recruit one guest at a time, and ask each of them if there are any individuals they do not want to work with. So far, the worst I've had to deal with is a guest not wanting to be seated near another guest at the VIP dinner, which isn't a difficult request to handle. However, at other cons, I have seen guests cancel their entire appearance due to a conflict with another guest.

Guests have different preferences when it comes to autograph sessions. Some want a permanent table or booth where they can sit whenever they aren't hosting a panel or other commitment. They like the un-structured nature of the all-day table where fans can approach them and spend time talking to them. Others will not want a dedicated table. They prefer to do scheduled autograph sessions. During these scheduled signing sessions, the crowd of fans can be controlled and regulated in a line so that each attendee only gets a short time with the celebrity. This is not only a decision that should be based on the scheduling and space restrictions of the convention, but you should definitely ask the guest what their preference is up front when initially negotiating their appearance. Some may be offended if they are used to having a dedicated table, but are not given one at your con. If a dedicated table is simply not reasonably doable at your convention, telling the guest up front will at the very least avoid any hurt feelings by tempering their expectations.

The final point on guests is that you need to treat them all equally. It is true that some guests are worth more than others. Some will sell a lot more tickets for you than others will. You are going to pay them different amounts based on that value. However, once the negotiations are done and the contracts are signed, they are all guests. Treat them all the same. If you take your guest of honor to dinner, take them all to dinner. If you treat them differently, it will be noticed. It will become obvious that you think of some of your guests as second class, and that kind of thing can get around, making it difficult to get more guests next year. On the other hand, taking all your guests out for dinner or lunch together is a really enjoyable experience. Make it a benefit for your staff as well. Having a dinner the night before the convention where you take all the guests out to eat and have your staff join them is good in so many ways. It's a huge reward for the staff, which makes them feel valued. It lets the guests meet the people who will be running the show, so they know at least the faces of the people in charge of different departments. And finally, the guests themselves will have a fantastic time, and if you're contractually required to pay for their meals anyway, might as well use it to your advantage. But the bottom line is, what you do for one, you should do for all.

The big-name guests probably expect it anyway, and the less famous ones will definitely sing the praises of your con to their friends and co-workers, which makes them all want to be guests at your con next year.

Exhibitors

Some of the first real revenue that will flow into your convention will be from exhibitors. They will begin signing up several months before the convention. The following are some tips for dealing with exhibitors, both from my experience as an exhibitor and as a convention organizer.

The first thing you need to know about exhibitors is that they are a significant part of why attendees come to a convention. Shopping is as much a draw for the crowd as the programming is. Keep that in mind the whole time. The vendors may be selling figurines and plushies, but you are selling access to the vendors. That's why people are buying tickets. For that reason, make sure to get the vendors to agree not to take down their booths early. They WILL try to begin loading out early on the last day if you let them. But as long as people are still paying to get in, the vendors need to be at their tables.

Think of it from the perspective of the attendees. They paid for the privilege of shopping at your event. If the dealers and artists close their booths early, the attendees aren't getting what they paid for. I had this problem the first year of Tiger Con, but for the second year, as part of their application form, I required all exhibitors to agree to remain set up until the end of business hours. Year two worked much better.

There are three basic types of exhibitors. Vendors, artists, and fans. Vendors (also called dealers) are selling retail merchandise. This is officially licensed products like you would find at a brick and mortar store in the mall, but obviously their products will be more focused on the specific target audience of your convention. These are businesses trying to make money. Typical booth spaces are 10'x10' and include two exhibitor passes, two chairs, and a number of tables (often only one). These are usually the most expensive spaces you will be selling. One issue with dealers is bootleg merchandise. If you've ever shopped on eBay for figurines, plushies, DVD/Blu-rays, etc., you've seen some rare ones that cost hundreds of dollars, but you can find (nearly) identical ones for extremely cheap. These are bootleg copies, and the copyright owners may even try to hold you responsible if you allow them to be sold at your event. You should make sure your dealer policies include a prohibition on bootleg merchandise.

Next are the artists. These are individuals selling their own work. They sell books, comics, art prints, pins, buttons, clothing, etc. The difference is that the items they sell must be made by them. They should not be allowed to re-sell items made by others, or mass produced merchandise. You should make this explicitly clear in the contract or application process. A typical artist alley space is a six or eight foot long table, chair, and a single exhibitor pass. They also usually make a lot less profit than a dealer or vendor, so you should charge significantly less for an artist table than a dealer booth. Some art may cross the line into bootleg or copyright violation, but since the artwork is done by the individual, it's a much harder distinction to make. A general rule of thumb is that fan art is acceptable as long as it isn't a direct copy of the original. They must add their own touch, unique style, or transform the work in some way. If the artist is simply reproducing a copyrighted symbol or logo, then that is probably a violation of the rule, and you can expect the copyright owner to complain if they find out about it. Usually they file the complaint directly with the artist, but they may go through you, the convention organizer, also.

Finally, fan tables are usually free tables where organizations can advertise. Other conventions are the usual customer for these tables, but they can also be for fan clubs or special interest groups. They will hand out promotional items and flyers to drum up interest for whatever they are advertising. Whether or not you allow them to sell items or hold a raffle to raise money is entirely up to you. In my experience, most conventions are fine with it as long as the revenue goes to fund the convention or organization hosting the table. It should not be a for-profit situation where a person or small group is keeping the money for personal gain. In that case, they should get an artist or dealer space. Some other conventions are of the opinion that you didn't pay for the space, so you shouldn't be making any money with it. In that case, no raffles may be held nor donations accepted by the group hosting the fan table. As the convention organizer, it will be up to you to set this rule.

Even if your convention is brand new, with no reputation or track record, exhibitors will want to be a part of it. So long as you put a reasonable price on the space, you should have no problem attracting more than you can fit in your space. The exhibitor application form should be one of the first working components of your website. As long as you have listed your convention with the appropriate online convention databases, and your website and social media pages look professional, the exhibitors will flock to you.

Because of this, you should be prepared to tell most of them "no." You will almost certainly get more applicants than you can possibly accept. Your goal should be to achieve a wide variety of merchandise for your attendees to shop. You may be tempted to simply approve applications as they come in, but the best way to do it is to jury the applicants. By that I mean take all the applicants and compare them to ensure you get high quality vendors selling a variety of different items. You can have one jury session for all the applicants, or you can do multiple sessions over time.

Advertising

Getting the word out about your new convention can be a challenge. Some methods of advertising are more effective than others. Hopefully, this section will keep you from wasting your advertising dollars.

As mentioned previously, fan tables are one of the most effective means of advertising. However, you should consider two factors when selecting which conventions to set up tables at. First is timing. If you hand someone a flyer for your convention and it doesn't happen until next year, that flyer will likely end up in the trash. Nobody is going to remember your flyer six months from now, and very few people are going to go buy a ticket with half a year or more before the doors open. The closer to the date of your convention you can get those flyers into people's hands, the more likely they will actually translate into ticket sales. The second factor is distance. Very few people will drive more than six hours for a first year con. It does happen, but it's not worth spending your advertising budget on. Focus on a reasonable driving distance and only do fan tables at conventions within that radius.

Flyers are great for getting the word out. A tri-fold flyer with all your guests, contests, etc., does build excitement, but they can be expensive. A simple business card with the name of your con, date, location, a picture of your mascot, and list of your guests costs about five cents per card. At the time of writing this book, Vistaprint has been doing a 500 card deal for about $25. Office Max, Staples, and other office supply sources can also produce large volumes of business cards at very reasonable prices, especially if you order online and pick up in the store.

Google AdWords and Facebook Ads seem like an attractive option. They sometimes offer a certain amount of free advertising to new users. They offer customization of your target audience as well as geographical targeting. That lets you limit the area in which the ad will appear and also limit it to those people who search for topics related to your con's theme. After your free advertising runs out, you will pay per click. You can adjust the setting to get different prices per click, but consider that the majority of people who click on your link are just getting information and not buying tickets. Pay close attention to what is called the conversion rate, which is the percentage of visitors who actually purchase something. In my experience, this type of advertising is a net loss for young or first year conventions. If you do use it, be sure to focus tightly on the target audience, and just like a fan table, only advertise close to your location geographically, and only for a limited time. I would advise only advertising by this method for a month before the con, two at the most.

One very effective means of advertising which costs very little money and gets a lot of results is visiting fan clubs within driving distance of the con. Libraries, schools, and universities are the usual places you will find a club. An internet search can yield some promising leads in this area, especially visiting the websites of the schools and libraries in the area to see if they have a listing of clubs which meet there. Contact the head of the club and set up a time to put on a presentation for the members. If they have a projector or large TV, make a presentation with all the pertinent info about your con. Make sure to solicit for volunteers. These clubs are filled with people who are obviously interested in and motivated to support your event.

Also try to get in on any local festivals or community events. Setting up a table at one of these can provide some of the best advertising for your dollar. Members of the local community are easier to convince to attend your event because they don't have to drive. If you are going to hand out actual flyers, this is where you will get the best return on your investment.

Management

Having great ideas is useless if you don't communicate them. Having a plan for a fantastic convention is worthless if you can't put together a team to execute it. As a leader, you have to inspire those who work for you. As mentioned before, leadership is getting people to want to do what you want them to do. Notice that it isn't simply getting people to do something. The essential ingredient is that they want to do it as much as you want them to do it. Sure, you may be able to power your way through putting on a con with sheer force of will, but if your staff is as invested as you are, they will make it so much easier for you. Someone who comes up with an improved way to do a job is much better than someone who just gets the job done. A staff member who actively seeks out problems is better than one who fixes problems after they occur.

The key to getting them to want to do what you want them to do is communication. You must share your vision with them, tell them how they fit into the overall success or failure of the plan, and empower them to solve problems. They have to feel like this is as much their convention as it is yours. When they take ownership, they make better decisions. To do this, you need to have regular meetings. Online messaging is great. You can set up an instant messaging group for your staff and they can share ideas at any time of the day or night, but it isn't as good as getting together face to face. Ideas flow much easier when you don't have to type them out.

Having a meeting once a month is fine so long as you have six months or more before the con. However, when you get inside six months, you need to meet more often. Twice a month is good when you have between six and two months to go. Eventually, somewhere between one or two months before the con, you should switch to weekly get-togethers. Have an agenda. Write down exactly what you want to talk about, but don't get upset if the topics wander. Let your people throw out ideas and let others shoot them down. This is the marketplace of ideas, and the strongest ones will float to the top. Hopefully, the bad ideas will sink. However, you do need to bring them back to the agenda when the discussion digresses too far or becomes non-productive. Write down all the good ideas that are put forward and assign a person to implement that idea as soon as it is agreed upon. Ideally, whoever came up with that idea should be put in charge of it unless it definitely falls into another staff member's purview. For instance, a great marketing idea should definitely be given to the public relations officer to work. When possible, giving the project to the one who suggested it is good because they will likely take ownership and not put it off as a burden which never gets completed. No matter what, never agree on a course of action without assigning someone to take charge of it. A great idea without a leader to head it up will simply be forgotten. You can't do everything yourself, so delegate.

The most important thing to remember about delegation is that you can delegate authority, but you can never delegate responsibility. You can empower someone to do a task with all the authority that you have. If you are in charge of the money, you can delegate your authority to spend it to another individual. However, if that person abuses that authority, the responsibility for the abuse is still yours. You are in charge of the money, and your choice to delegate to an irresponsible assistant was the reason for the abuse. For that reason, follow up with your appointees. You don't need to watch their every move. Nobody likes having a micromanager for a boss. However, you do need to check in regularly to make sure the job is getting done and that it is being done the way you intended. My recommendation is to clearly set up your expectations when you assign the task. Check with them about half way through the job to make sure it's on course. And finally, check on it again when you judge that it should be complete or nearly complete.

Delegating authority is, as you can guess, a double-edged sword. It means you don't have to be present and make every decision. It lets you get more done, but it also introduces an element of risk. The risk is that something will not get done or that it will get done wrong. One way to minimize the risk is to establish a direct chain of authority so that you can ensure that your vision is executed at every level. This is called a chain of command, and it begins with you, the convention organizer or chairperson. Beneath you are your officers, or department heads. The treasurer, public affairs director, director of operations, and guest relations director all answer directly to you. Beneath them are several officers and appointees, also known as front line supervisors, who answer to the officers. From the top down it is chairman at the top, upper management beneath the chairman, possibly some middle managers, and finally, front-line supervisors leading groups of workers.

As time progresses, the number of staff will increase. For example, one person can probably handle the entire treasurer position by themselves at first, but eventually you may appoint an officer specifically in charge of fundraising, or you may even break it up into sub departments with one person in charge of recruiting sponsors, and another responsible for promotions such as merchandising and fundraisers (raffles, etc.), and one to handle vendors and artists. Beneath the public affairs director you may want to appoint officers to handle your online presence, fan tables and physical advertising, etc. The guest relations director will definitely need to appoint a guest liaison for each of your guests.

The most important department which needs to have front line supervisors is operations. Ops covers a lot of things. Basically, everything that happens *at the convention* falls under operations. This department is responsible for setting the schedule and making sure it all happens on time and in the right place. Sub categories of this department include security, tech support, logistics, setup and cleanup. You can imagine how difficult it would be for a single person to oversee all of this, so they will definitely need to appoint front line supervisors.

The front line supervisor is the person who knows how things need to be done and directs individual workers to make it so. One example is setup. If you are setting up a stage, pipe and drape, tables, chairs, etc., the director of operations can brief one supervisor for each of these tasks with his vision of how it should be set up, and then the supervisor can make sure the five or ten volunteers doing the job get it done right. The director doesn't need to be present, and is free to handle any problems which pop up, and they will. The treasurer will likewise appoint supervisors for at-the-door ticket sales and badge pickup.

The flow should be direct. The chairman tells the director what needs to be done. The director decides how to do that and tells the supervisor. Finally, the supervisor ensures that the volunteers and workers do it the way the director wants. Obviously, smaller conventions will have fewer managers and supervisors, with the directors overseeing things personally while larger conventions may even add another level of management entirely. No matter what the size of your convention, a chain of command like this makes it so that nobody is confused about who to go to with questions, and it ensures that two people aren't simultaneously making conflicting decisions and duplicating effort.

Job descriptions:

Chairperson: Carries the ultimate responsibility for the success or failure of the convention. The chairperson must communicate the vision for how the convention will be run. This is the decision maker. The chairperson assigns duties to the other officers and monitors to make sure those duties are executed correctly. During the convention, this is the busiest staff member. The chairperson normally is out visiting every part of the convention, spending a few minutes at each area to make sure everything is running correctly.

Treasurer: Keeps detailed records of money in/out, approves purchases and sets limits. Responsible for managing ticket sales, but may delegate to more tech savvy individuals, especially for online sales. Also responsible for acquiring sponsors, but this could also fall under Public Relations.

Public Relations: Responsible for advertising and promoting the con. Manages online presence as well as physical promotional items. Responsible for creating the program guide. Along with the Chairperson, meets with community organizations. Responsible for signs and banners on the day of the con. Highly advised to delegate a lieutenant to handle/recruit sponsors.

Programming Director: Sets the schedule and assigns room space. Makes sure everything runs on time with no conflicts. The schedule needs to be finalized in time to include it in the program guide and have the guide produced before the convention begins.

Guest Relations: Communicates with guests prior to con. Develops guest contracts and works to meet them. Reserves transportation and lodging for guests. Makes gift bags for guests. Sets up green room. Assigns a liaison to each guest.

Guest Liaison: Personal assistant to an individual guest. Shadows the guest during the con. Makes sure the guests are at all of their appearances on time. Makes sure the guests are fed and happy. Basically a gofer for the guest.

Volunteer Coordinator: Handles volunteer registration. Assigns volunteers to tasks/shifts. Briefs volunteers on duties. Makes sure volunteers are doing their jobs correctly.

Vendor Relations Liaison: This officer has two jobs. First, before the con, they are in charge of dealer and artist alley applications and selecting who gets a table or booth. They may also handle dealer contracts if you choose to have contracts. Second, during the con, they are in charge of setting up the vending areas and making sure each vendor knows where their assigned space is. They also check on the vendors periodically during the event to make sure there are no problems.

Operations Director: Works directly with the Programming Director and Logistics Director to ensure everything happens on time. Makes sure panel/event rooms are set up correctly and ready for the next event. Makes sure equipment is in the correct place for the events which need them. Basically, this person is an assistant-chairperson who takes some of the burden of problem solving off of the chairperson's shoulders. The chairman cannot be everywhere solving every emergency that comes up. The operations director can do a lot of that. The difference between the chairperson and the operations director is that the operations director is primarily concerned with executing the schedule, whereas the chairperson is focused on the big picture and oversees all the other officers and makes decisions about policies and the convention in general.

Security Chief: This job can be a subset of the volunteer director. The security chief manages all the security volunteers to make sure all shifts are filled. It is advised to have two tiers of security volunteers. The lowest level are just badge checkers. They stand outside the panel rooms and dealer areas to make sure everyone has and displays their proof of payment, whether that be a wristband or a badge. Top tier volunteers are the ones you trust implicitly with the authority to deal with unruly attendees. Depending on how much you trust top tier security, you may delegate authority to remove attendees from the convention, or you may retain that authority for the security chief only. Top tier security should have some means of communication, i.e. cellphone or radio.

Logistics Director: This is the person responsible for getting all the stuff to and from the convention. They primarily work the day before the con and the day after. They pick up and transport all the rented equipment, such as tables, chairs, stage, canopies for outdoor activities, signs, banners, speakers and sound systems, etc. They coordinate the number of vehicles required, and make sure the drivers know when and where to go. The logistics director can also be responsible for setup of the venue before the con and cleanup afterwards.

Prize Manager: This officer is responsible for keeping and organizing all the prizes for the various contests. Sponsors love to give prizes, and someone needs to keep track of them all and assign prizes to the various contests. You may need prizes for each category in your AMV contest, cosplay contest, video game tournament, raffles, etc. It is important to ensure that sponsors get credit for donated prizes. The prize manager can be a huge help in keeping track of this and making sure they are announced at the various contests. This officer can also be put in charge of creating the gift bags for each of your guests of honor, and swag bags for VIP attendees.

Gaming Director: This officer is in charge of the tabletop and video gaming events. They set times for contests and tournaments, and arrange for people to run them. The video game room tends to get quite messy if not constantly monitored. The gaming director keeps this part of the con running smoothly.

Entertainment director: If you have any music or performance events, they will be the responsibility of the entertainment director. Tiger Con had live music, a rave, and a cosplay tap dance performance. These groups usually have specific requirements for equipment, etc. Having a single point of contact for all of your performers/entertainers is a good idea.

Tech Support: Panelists will have trouble hooking up their laptops, musicians will have trouble using the sound system, the projector will have unexpected quirks, etc. Having a tech-savvy volunteer in each panel room to assist panelists is a great idea if you have enough skilled volunteers. If not, at least have one person who is familiar with your equipment and is designated to deal with these problems.

<h3 style="text-align:center">Holding a Staff Meeting:</h3>

Even if you are using some type of instant messaging service to keep all staff members in contact with each other, it is essential to have a structured meeting where everyone gets together face to face to discuss the progress being made. You don't necessarily need PowerPoint slides to bore everyone to death, but you do need to conduct some essential business. My recommendation is to follow this format:

Before the meeting, while people are showing up, provide something entertaining for people to enjoy. Playing the Anime Music Videos which have been submitted for the AMV contest since the last meeting is always fun. It also builds excitement among the staff. Keeping people positive about the event is essential because everyone wants to be on a winning team. That's how you get the best quality work out of your people.

Make sure you have someone performing the role of secretary or scribe to record the meeting. Being able to review the minutes, especially when you can't remember who you assigned a specific task to, or what the result of a certain vote was, is a tremendous help.

Call the meeting to order and go over the news. Share what you as the chairperson and the group in general have achieved since the last meeting. Major policy decisions, updates from the venue, new guests etc. Solicit any needed volunteers to man fan tables at upcoming events or appoint new officers.

The most important part of the meeting is to have each officer give an update on what they have been working on, what they still need to do, and what they need help with. You can have a list, perhaps on a slide, or you can go around the room. Either way, get each officer to report on their progress, successes, and issues/problems.

In the end, hand out any new assignments for your officers to complete. Be sure to give them a deadline. Even if it's a simple thing that can be done easily and quickly, give them a timeframe of when you expect it to be done. Projects without a due date tend to get forgotten. Ask if there is any additional/new business, and then close the meeting.

While it's not essential, I always offer some type of entertainment to follow the business of the meeting. Gaming, movie, food, etc. This too helps to keep people motivated. It makes the task of attending a meeting feel more like a privilege than a chore. Of course, this comes down to knowing your audience. If you are a club on a college, running a small convention in your student union, this format works great. If, on the other hand, you are a group of 30 or 40 somethings with executive experience, planning a for-profit convention as a business venture, then the motivation part is less important. For a group like the latter, you may want to stick with Robert's Rules for meetings, which will inspire confidence by appealing to their professional nature.

Chain of Command

My background is military. 24 years in the Air Force has shaped my opinion on how to run an organization. There are many different organizational structures you can chose from, but the linear hierarchy has certain advantages that I have come to appreciate, and I think you will too. While matrix and other de-centralized structures may work well for large, geographically spread out organizations, and they may empower managers at various levels, even the largest convention is really a small organization compared to most corporations. Many would go with a democratic style organization where the major decisions are determined by a group vote. While this may empower your members and give them a sense of ownership, I would caution against using this style of management. Giving decision making power to those who face no consequences in the case of failure can be dangerous. Also, your goal is focused and time dependent. Everything has to happen in a certain order to make a very specific deadline. Sometimes you just need a decision made quickly. Because of this, a command style bureaucracy works best.

At the top is the chairperson, or president, who has ultimate responsibility. If you're funding this thing, then the buck definitely stops with you, but even if the money comes from somewhere else, you are the person most responsible for the success or failure of the event, so you should have the final say on any major decision. This is not to say you can't open up decisions to a vote, just keep the all-or-nothing, success-or-failure decisions restricted to those members (or member) who will shoulder the burden if it falls apart. If the decision is which guest of honor to invite, that's a great democratic decision to put to a vote. If the decision is whether or not to include a rave at your event, then you may want to weigh that one yourself. A rave comes with a lot of risk, and is difficult or impossible to insure. You could find yourself in legal or financial trouble if things go badly. Ask your staff for input, but make the final decision yourself.

One way to organize the chain of command is to divide it into staff and operations. The staff are primarily planners whose jobs are mostly done before the convention. The operations side of the chain is primarily concerned with what happens on the day of the convention. They execute the plan developed by the staff.

Below the chairperson on the operations side is your director of operations. This could even be a co-chairperson. If you go with a co-chair, then they will be like a vice-president. You are still ultimately responsible, but this trusted agent can take some of the burden of monitoring and guiding the staff and even hosting meetings when you are not available. Alternately, a director of operations is only responsible for operations. They execute the plan that has been set. They aren't really concerned with the planning, budgeting, scheduling, etc. Rather, their job is mostly to take that plan, which is developed by the staff, and make it happen efficiently and on time. You will delegate a lot of tasks to this person. You will often give your director of ops instructions like, "Go to X and make sure Y is happening. Y is our top priority, so pull volunteers from Z if you need to."

Beneath the director of operations are the front line managers whose jobs are done primarily during the execution of the convention. Security, Volunteer Coordinator, Logistics Director, Prize Manager, Gaming Director, Entertainment Director, and Tech Support. They answer directly to the Director of Operations, and that creates a filter which keeps every small question and concern from making its way up to the chairperson.

You should give every manager, especially the director of operations, clear guidelines on how much authority they have. For instance, you could say that as long as the decision doesn't cost money or reflect on the public image of the convention, the director of operations has full authority to make the decision. Or, for lower level managers such as programming director, you could say that as long as the decision doesn't affect any other department, then the decision falls within the programming director's authority to make. There is some gray area in the latter. The programming director may want to reschedule the costume contest to be right after the music video contest, or to move it from Saturday to Sunday. At first, this would seem to be a decision which only affects programming, however, it could potentially affect vending and public image as well. Main events such as the music video and costume contest draw a significant portion of your attendees. I have had dealers complain that there weren't enough attendees shopping to make it worth their time.

However, there were plenty of attendees at the convention. They were all crowded into the AMV and costume contests which I had allowed to be scheduled back to back and the dealer room suffered because many of their potential customers were at the two main events for an extended time. Moving a main event from one day to another could also potentially affect the public image of the convention. For some people, the costume contest is the primary reason for attending a convention. If they bought a Saturday only ticket, and now the primary thing they want to attend is moved to Sunday, they could leave a bad review for your event. In both cases, what seems like a purely scheduling decision affected other departments, so be careful.

The managers will often need more and more people underneath them as the day of the event approaches. The treasurer will need additional people to help manage the registration booth. Volunteers should not normally be trusted with money. Only members of your organization who you trust should handle money. Guest relations will need individual liaisons for each guest. Of course security and logistics will need large numbers of workers to get the job done.

Questions flow up the chain. If the workers have questions, they ask their front line managers. If the managers have questions, they can ask the director of operations. If the director of operations isn't comfortable making the final call, then the problem is taken to the chairperson.

Going down the chain works similarly. The chairperson may check on a panel room to find that it is late getting started because the panelist is having trouble hooking up their laptop to the projector. As the chairperson, you shouldn't be the one helping the panelist. You have bigger things to worry about. You should contact the director of operations and tell them of the delay in panel room #1 and that tech support is needed. The director will tell tech support, and they should fix the problem. The director of operations should then follow up by checking to make sure the problem got corrected in a reasonable amount of time. The director of operations is your fire-and-forget weapon. No need to check on this again, the director has full authority to handle it. Likewise, if the chairperson notices the need for a policy change that affects multiple departments, it should flow down through the director of operations to the front line managers and finally to the workers and volunteers. You can't tell everyone, or at least that would be an inefficient use of your time, so use the chain of command to get the word out.

On the other side of the chain is the staff or administration side, as opposed to the operations side. It is composed of the chairperson's support staff. These are the managers primarily responsible for creating the plan. Contracts, money, schedules, documents, advertising, etc., come from this side of the chain. While they will have things to do during the convention, their primary role is in the lead-up to the con. Treasurer, Public Relations, Guest Relations, Vendor Relations, Programming Director, etc. fall under this chain. They report directly to the chair or co-chair. These are make-or-break positions which the chairperson needs a direct line of authority to. You may notice that all of these positions are tied to the money. The operations side of the chart is doing the heavy lifting; making the event actually happen. The admin side of the chart is planning and paying for the event. Public relations is getting people to buy tickets, guest relations is making deals and contracts with guests, vendor relations is selling artist alley tables and dealer booths, and the programming director is making sure things are happening that people will want to attend. Of course some of these positions, such as vendor relations, will transition to the operations side of the organization during the actual convention.

One last note. Having a co-chair or director of operations is crucial if you, the chairperson, will be hosting any events during the convention. Especially if you are hosting any events featuring your special guests. It is probably best if you appoint someone else to host these events, but you are definitely going to want to speak during the opening and closing ceremonies, and possibly some other main events. It can delay the event and begin to affect the schedule if your staff interrupts you with questions or emergencies while you are hosting, especially if you are hosting an event featuring a guest of honor. It could offend your guest if you have to pause the presentation to handle other business. Having a competent co-chair or director of operations can really save the day in this area.

Managing Disputes

Managing personal disputes is an essential skill for convention organizers. You will experience conflicts with and between guests, attendees, volunteers and staff. This is by far the most stressful part of the job. For some reason it is easier, emotionally, to deal with disasters such as damaged equipment, cancelled guests, or schedule conflicts than it is to deal with personal disputes between staff members. This may be because most of the former are unavoidable or unforeseeable. They just happen. Personality conflicts are completely under the control of the people who participate in them. Two people can work together, especially for a single weekend, despite an abiding dislike for each other, if they are professionals. They may truly detest each other, but the decision to engage in disruptive behavior is a choice they make. When the individuals are on your own staff, it makes it even more stressful because these staff members know just what is at stake and how their behavior will affect the event as a whole. Their failure to put the success of the event above their personal feelings represents a betrayal of all those who worked so hard to put the event on. As difficult as it is to believe that your staff or volunteers would do this, you will almost certainly have to deal with this as a convention organizer.

Personality conflicts can take several forms. From two individuals who simply demand not to be in the same room with each other, to active sabotage of the other person's efforts in order to damage their reputation. In severe cases, such as the latter, it is better to simply go short handed on your staff than to allow in-fighting to bring down the convention. You must weigh the potential damage caused by losing a staff member who has corporate knowledge which allows them to perform their duties, against the potential damage of allowing them to stay and bring down the efforts of another department. If you can do without them, and it is clear that they are the source of the problems, then it is best to dismiss them. This will not only remove a disruptive element, but it will also send a strong message that this type of immaturity will not be tolerated.

There are several ways of dealing with these types of personality conflicts. What follows is simply my technique, and it has worked well for me in the past. You may decide to go with what has worked for you, but whichever technique you use, it must be tempered with the knowledge that when the conflict is between two people, neither will usually give you the whole truth. Both parties will usually present you with some version of the truth which presents themselves as the victim. The truth is somewhere in the middle. It is best to gather as much information as possible before engaging either party. Ask witnesses, especially disinterested third parties. Observe both parties before attempting to intervene.

Step one is to speak with them individually. Bringing them both together for some type of mediation in the middle of the chaos of an ongoing convention is a terrible idea. Your goal should not be to resolve their differences. Your goal should be to return the convention to smooth operation. The conflict can be addressed later, when the success of the convention is not on the line.

Always begin by asking, not telling. Let them tell you what the problem is. They will be more receptive to you if you show interest in them as a person. You may not be able to do anything about the perceived wrong they have suffered, but you can listen to their point of view. Once they have aired their grievance, let them know that you understand how they feel, but there's almost nothing that can be done about it immediately. Your goal should be a truce. Get both parties to agree to table their differences until after the convention. If either party refuses to let it go for now and address it later, **they should be removed**. If they lack the maturity to put the mission (a successful convention) before their feelings, then they are a liability. Even replacing them with another person who doesn't fully understand the job is preferable to having someone actively seeking to damage the operation of the convention.

In the case of guests who have personality conflicts, it can be even more complicated, but it rarely gets as bad as ones between staff. Where guests are concerned, people have paid for the opportunity to meet them at your convention. Removing a guest can upset a lot of people. It is the absolute last resort. You should do everything within reason to accommodate a guest who has a personality conflict with another guest or staff member. Rearrange the schedule or make changes to the layout of the convention (i.e. move an autograph table to another part of the con in order to keep the two guests apart) if necessary. Fortunately, this type of conflict, while not uncommon, is usually the easiest to deal with. Most guests, even when they truly dislike another guest, will behave professionally and not let on to attendees that they have a problem. At the worst, they will complain to you as the convention organizer and try to get some accommodation which will keep them separated from each other, or they will cancel their appearance in advance. They are extremely unlikely to behave unprofessionally in front of fans.

When attendees are the problem, it can still be tricky to deal with. Simply banning a disruptive attendee is more complicated than you might think. In the age of social media, a single individual can have a very loud voice. The reason you asked them to leave may have been perfectly appropriate, but they are probably going to say negative things about the convention on all of their social media outlets. Keep this in mind when banning an attendee. My advice is not to engage in any kind of discourse with the individual online. If you respond to them, it keeps the conversation going. You want the issue to disappear, and arguing with them does the opposite. Let them say their piece. Put out a statement if you feel it to be absolutely necessary to clear up the situation, and then let it go. Let the post get buried in the hundreds of other posts online and soon people will forget about it. The legality of banning an attendee can vary from state to state, but in general if you rent a space (such as a convention center) then you have the right to ask someone to leave, and if they do not, they are trespassing. It is no different than renting a hotel room, and someone refusing to leave your room. You can call the authorities to have them removed if necessary.

Legal

Disclaimer: I am not a lawyer, and this is not official legal advice. This is just a list of things which I have dealt with as a convention organizer that I think first time organizers should be aware of.

There's a lot to talk about in this area, and how much of it applies to you will depend on the size and frequency of your event. You may not need all of these items, particularly the tax and licensing part if your event is small, with only a hundred or so attendees. The same can be said if it's a one-time only thing. If you don't plan to make it a recurring convention, then a lot of this advice may not apply. For example, with the first year of Tiger Con, we only had about 400 attendees. By comparison, some other organizations with which I have worked that held Christmas parties or award ceremonies with 500 or more attendees did not register or pay taxes on their ticket sales, but that's because those organizations were large and the Christmas party was not their main focus. For Tiger Con, certain tax requirements may not have applied if we had only held the convention a single time or if the convention was a small part of what our club did. However, because we were honest about our intentions to make the event a recurring event and the fact that the vast majority of our club funds were related to the convention, we were subject to those requirements. Just use some common sense and let your conscience guide you. If you aren't sure, seek actual legal advice from a lawyer or tax specialist. At the very least, read up on the rules at the IRS website (include link).

The first and arguably most important thing you need to do is to protect yourself. If someone gets hurt at your event, even through no fault of your own, it can be a costly situation to deal with. Event insurance is an inexpensive way to shield yourself against this. Event insurance can even cover some situations that you may not expect, such as breach of contract or defamation of character. You will likely have many different contracts, such as vendor contracts, guest contracts, perhaps a contract with your venue or your entertainment (DJ, etc.). They can sue you if you don't live up to the terms of the agreement. A good event insurance policy will cover this. For Tiger Con, I was able to purchase two million dollars of event insurance for only $175. That's a small price tag for so much peace of mind. A quick Google search will turn up many companies offering event insurance. Shop around and compare policies. Make sure to read the details of the coverage. You will find that they often have clauses such as "No Raves" that can affect your event.

For a perfect example of why you need insurance, look up a convention called Rainfurrest. (https://www.youtube.com/watch?v=GmULc5VANsw) Conventions fail for a variety of reasons, usually bad management. However, in the case of Rainfurrest, it was the attendees who caused the con to fail. Out of control parties, trash everywhere, and damage to the venue made it so no other hotel or convention center would book Rainfurrest for a second year. This wasn't accidental damage, but intentional damage on the part of the attendees. Examples include leaving full diapers around the hotel and on cars in the parking lot, as well as filling the hot tub with towels and stuffing towels into the water pump until it failed. Venues can charge your organization for the repair costs if this happens.

Insurance doesn't cover everything. What if you overextend yourself financially? You should always plan to start small and grow, but if you do overbook on venue and guests and then can't sell enough tickets to pay the bills, you may be looking at legal trouble. The ultimate legal shield to protect yourself with is a Limited Liability Corporation or LLC.

It only costs around $100-$200 to form an LLC, and the paperwork is minimal. It can vary from state to state, but many do not require anything beyond an annual renewal, which is done

entirely online. Without getting too technical, forming an LLC
will protect your personal assets from legal liability. Since the
assets of the LLC are legally separate from the assets of the
owner, your home and personal finances are protected.
However, if you are the sole proprietor of the convention, as the
chairperson, you can be personally liable if something goes
wrong, and without an LLC, your personal property and finances
can be taken to pay for debts incurred by the convention. For
such a small price, this seems like a no-brainer for any
convention.

If you want to open a bank account or line of credit
specifically for the convention, then you may need an Employer
Identification Number. This is basically a tax identification
number for your convention. Banks will often ask for this if you
try to open an account in the convention's name rather than your
own. The benefit is that business accounts may have perks that a
personal account does not. The EIN is the means by which you
(or your LLC) will pay taxes on any profit made by the
convention, but it isn't necessarily complicated. In most cases,
as a sole proprietor, you just file the taxes with your personal tax
return. No need to hire a specialist as it's just not that
complicated, so long as you keep good records.

Sales tax is a more complicated issue. Technically, you do have to pay sales tax on your ticket sales. However, using a ticket service can simplify things. Online ticket sales will cross state lines. Different amounts of tax will apply. It can be a real mess. My advice is to find a ticket service that will handle all of that for you. If the company handling your ticket sales collects and pays your sales tax for you, then it takes a lot of burden off of you. Now the only sales tax you need to keep track of are the at-the-door sales, which is much less complicated because that, at least, is all taking place in one physical location and only one sales tax rate applies.

Depending on where you live, you can probably go online to your state or county tax office and apply for a license to sell, which will then give you a means to report and pay sales tax. There may also be a city sales tax as well. I wish I had better news for you, but you are just going to have to research the city, county, and state sales tax rules for yourself because they vary too much for my advice to be accurate for your situation. Fortunately, you can almost certainly find the info you need online.

You can possibly avoid the whole tax issue entirely by registering as a 501(c)(3) tax exempt organization. However, it's a bit more complicated than just filling out a form. Some conventions are able to register as tax exempt, while others are not. If it was an option available to everyone, most if not all conventions would opt for tax exempt status. The problem is that not every convention or organization qualifies for this status. It's also more difficult for comic or multi-genre conventions to get tax exempt. The ones who are able to pull it off are often the ones with a much tighter focus, such as anime conventions. This is because the IRS only extends this status to organizations which fall into the following categories:

- Religious.

- Charitable.

- Scientific.

- Testing for public safety.

- Literary.

- Educational.

- Fostering national or international amateur sports competition.

- The prevention of cruelty to children or animals.

You may be able to get an exemption for charity purposes if you donate your proceeds to a qualifying charity. One possibility is to make your event a charity fund raiser. If you opt to donate all proceeds above what you needed to pay your operating expenses to a charity such as the Wounded Warrior Foundation and the That Others May Live Foundation, you can then apply for tax exempt status under the charity category.

Some anime-specific conventions are able to make use of the educational category by offering many panels and classes which showcase Japanese culture, literary and film analysis, and language. If you have enough cultural and educational content, you might be able to get approved on that basis. Of course, this is harder to do with a multi-genre convention because the focus is more obviously on entertainment than education.

You should consider if the juice is worth the squeeze since registering for tax exempt status isn't free. It can cost between $400 and $750 depending on how much revenue your organization brings in. For a very small, first year convention, the money saved in taxes will likely be equal to or less than the filing fee. In which case, the only real benefit to filing is to avoid dealing with all those different tax situations involved with inter-state ticket and merchandise sales.

Contracts:

Don't let the idea of writing contracts intimidate you. There are plenty of examples online that you can use. Just google examples of convention guest contracts, convention dealer contracts, etc., and you will find plenty. Just modify them to fit your specific situation and you're ready to go.

There are three types of contracts you will be primarily concerned with, and only two of them will be written by you. Let's start with the one that you don't have much control over. The venue contract.

Convention centers and hotels may require you to sign a contract. I say "may" because not every venue will require it. Hotels may simply have you sign a sheet along with paying your deposit which states the policies of the venue. Usually this is nothing unreasonable; just policies which protect the venue such as a clause prohibiting putting up signs on the walls or defacing hotel property. They may include their cancellation policy, but they may not. Larger venues, such as proper convention centers, will have a multi-page contract for you to sign. Obviously you should read over this document carefully.

Items you should pay particular attention to are the payment schedule, the cancellation policy, discounts/credits, and staffing. The payment schedule may be staggered so you pay some now, some a few months before the con, and the rest after. It may be all up-front, or it may be a small deposit now, and the rest at the time of the convention. You may be able to negotiate a modification to the payment schedule, depending on how badly the venue wants to book you. It helps if you already have a track record (last year's attendance) to show that you can bring in the numbers.

The cancellation policy is often very generous to the venue. One policy I had to negotiate included a requirement to give six months' notice for cancellations. After six months, even if the event was cancelled, the convention was required to pay full price, even though the convention center was free to book the venue with another group and essentially get paid twice for the same date. Just like the payment schedule, I had some success in getting a more lenient cancellation policy. You never know if you can get what you want until you ask.

If they promise you any type of credit, such as for food sales or for hotel room blocks, that should be spelled out in writing. These things may be promised by a convention center staff member as much as a year before the con, and that staff member may either forget or get a new job and not tell their replacement about the deal that was made. Having it in writing is always best.

Finally, larger convention centers may have a clause about staffing. Make sure to take a close look at this. They may have specifications about security personnel and loading/unloading. Some convention centers may have their own, even unionized, team to setup the dealer room and load the dealers' merchandise into the hall. In at least one case I know of, this increased the price the dealers had to pay for their spaces in order to cover the cost of the loading team.

Don't be afraid to ask for the venue to make exceptions to their policies. The worst that can happen is they say no. Especially if the financial situation is such that you simply cannot make the payment schedule, they may be willing to modify that schedule rather than lose you as a client.

Guest contracts are a far more individual and customized thing than venue contracts. Many guests have a list of standard requirements. You should ask for this list up front before typing up a contract. They may specify such things as preferred airline or seating, dietary requirements or preferences, use of their name or likeness, per-diem, specifics of payment, and ground transportation preferences. Something you may be tempted to include is a non-competition clause. This will prohibit the guest from appearing at another convention within your local geographical area for a specified period of time. This makes it so that if the guest's fans want to meet them, they have to come to your event. If your guest is going to appear at another convention just an hour or two away from yours, then you probably won't get any attendees from that location to attend your con. Be careful when including such a clause because some guests have strong policies against signing any such agreement.

Vendor contracts are something that you may or may not need. I offer them on an as-requested basis. I have one ready to go, because some dealers or artists don't feel comfortable paying for a booth without a contract, but most don't care. You may already have a page of vendor and artist policies, including cancellation, refunds, damage to premises, etc., on your website. You can usually just take this, add a couple of items, and include a signature block to make an exhibitor contract. I have been an exhibitor at a dozen conventions, and I have only had to sign a contract for one of them, so they aren't very common except for at the largest of conventions. Just like with guest contracts, be careful about the inclusion of a non-competition clause. I very nearly cancelled my appearance at that convention because I didn't want to preclude myself from exhibiting at other cons in that area. However, that con was being run by a friend of mine and I would rather exhibit at his con than any of the others, so I signed it. Vendors which have no particular attachment to your event may turn you down rather than limit their options.

Policies

Just like with contracts, policies are a lot less difficult than you might think. I highly advise just going to the websites for several conventions similar to yours and reading their policies. See what they cover and write your policies to be similar, but of course tailored to your specific situation and venue. Reviewing other convention policies will help you to avoid missing an important category. Standard categories include: Photography, Advertising/Sales, Behavior, Costumes, Weapons, and Props.

There are three things you will want to address in your photography policies. First is to make sure that attendees know that cosplayers are just attendees like everyone else. They have the same rights and should be treated with respect. You should inform your attendees to ask before taking photographs of cosplayers. Second is to emphasize that photo shoots should not block traffic. Setting up lights and other equipment in high traffic areas should be avoided. And finally, the staff or even professional photographers hired by the staff may be taking pictures at the con. Attendees should be aware that by purchasing a ticket they are agreeing to be photographed by the convention for promotional use.

As for advertising and sales, you will want to restrict sales to approved vendors and artists. No selling outside of the designated vendor area. It isn't fair to the artists and dealers who have paid for the privilege of doing business at your convention if anyone is allowed to sell things. Similarly, many conventions have strict rules about advertising or putting up signs. Keep in mind that if you allow just anyone to put up a sign, it implies that the convention condones the message or supports the business on that sign.

Behavior is pretty straightforward, but sometimes you need to spell things out. Examples include hygiene, public inebriation (and similar intoxication), offensive language, and impeding traffic flow.

Costumes, weapons, and props should be covered in your policies. Define what is considered as indecent or too revealing for costumes. Also define how realistic of prop weapons will be accepted, and have a station for all props to be inspected by the staff before allowing them into the con.

You should also address the carrying of real weapons. There are many options to consider, such as simply stating that attendees must comply with all local, state, and federal laws concerning weapons. You may want to overtly state whether licensed concealed weapon permit holders are allowed to bring weapons. Keep in mind that laws concerning weapons vary significantly from state to state, or even city to city. For instance, in Arizona, at least when I lived there, businesses were allowed to prohibit weapons, but they were required to provide secure storage for any weapons that their customers were required to relinquished. Also, at the time of writing this book, businesses in the state of Georgia may post notices that weapons are not allowed on the premises, however, such signs are not legally enforceable. The best course of action when drafting your weapons policy is to consult either a lawyer or a firearms instructor. Both are likely to have detailed knowledge of the local rules.

The other category of live weapon that you should address is swords. Many conventions have vendors who sell bladed weapons. You may want to require these weapons to remain in their original packaging, or you may require them to be removed from the premises after purchase. At the very least, you should probably prohibit any type of horseplay or mock-fighting with these weapons. I would advise limiting weapon handling, even prop weapons, to static poses for photography. Even allowing "slow motion" fighting is problematic, since "slow" is a very subjective term.

To ensure that everyone is aware of the policies and agrees to abide by them, you can add an, "Agree to Policies" button to your pre-registration form on your ticketing service, and also include the policies in the program guide for those who purchase tickets at the door.

Timeline

The following is a general guide on when certain tasks should be completed. There is of course some flexibility, and you can adjust it to suit your specific needs. However, one thing you will note is that the work load increases as time goes by. You can expect to spend two or three hours per week working on your convention when you have six months or more until the doors open. However, when you are three to six months out, you will probably be spending at least some time, about an hour, on con business every single day. When you are down to a month or just a few weeks to go, you will probably spend a majority of each day doing convention business. Plan on some late nights, and you may not sleep at all the weekend of the con.

One Year Out:

- o Appoint Main Officers (Chair, Treasurer, Public Relations)
- o Pick a Name
- o Register for an Employer Identification Number

o Set Up Bank/Credit Accounts

o Pick a Date

o Reserve a Location

10 Months Out:

o Create a Website

o Get Listed on Convention Databases

o Create Social Media Outlets

o Set Up Ticketing Site/Service

o Open registration for Attendees/Artists/Vendors/Panelists/Volunteers

o Execute Advertising Campaign (Promotional Items, Fan Tables, etc.)

o Appoint Staff Officers (Programming Director, Guest Relations, Vendor Relations)

o Set Up LLC/Business License

o Invite and Confirm Guests

o Purchase Event Insurance

o Recruit Sponsors

Six Months Out:

o Appoint Minor Officers

o Reserve any Needed Rentals (Chairs/Tables/Lighting/Stage/etc.)
o Face to Face Advertising (Fan Tables, Festivals, Handing Out Flyers)

Three Months Out:

o Book Guest Airfare/Travel

o Reserve Hotel Rooms for Guests, etc.

o Book entertainment (DJ, Event Hosts, Contest Judges, Professional Panelists)

o Book VIP dinner and any other food/entertainment reservations

o Book Guest Travel Arrangements

o Select Panelists

o Draft the Schedule

o Draft the Program Guide

o Create Badges (or purchase wristbands)

Make sure you have more than you think you will need. You are still at least a month from the event, and most of your ticket sales will happen in this time period. Be prepared for a good sized crowd. Better to have too many than too few badges/wristbands.

o Meet with venue staff to discuss expectations.

If the venue has never hosted a fandom convention they may not be familiar with the types of programming you will be hosting. You should definitely discuss specifics such as food for the VIP dinner or maid café. If you are planning a rave, the venue should know. They may have noise restrictions, etc., which may affect concerts or raves. You should also discuss banners and signs you would like to set up, as they may have rules about this as well.

o Appoint Operations Staff (Logistics, Prize Manager, Gaming Director, Entertainment Director, Tech Support)
o Increase staff meeting frequency to every other week.

Issues will come up at an increased rate, and more communication is better. Especially with limited time to address these issues.

One to Two Months out:

o If you are going to use them, this is the time to start online advertising (Google AdWords, etc.)
o Finalize the schedule.
o Produce the Program Guide.
o Email Each Guest a Personalized Schedule
o Appoint Guest Liaisons

- o Produce banners and signs which will be set up at the venue.

Printing may be quick, but same as with the program guide, delays can happen. Don't wait till the last minute.

- o Staff Tour of Venue

Take all staff to tour the venue to see where they will be working. Being familiar with the building the convention will take place in is extremely helpful in planning, and in describing what you want done with the space and how it should be used.

- o Create Certificates/Trophies for Contests

One or Two Weeks Prior:

- o Create gift bags for guests.
- o Perform a Staff Tabletop Timeline Walkthrough

You should have all available staff and volunteers meet and go over what will happen from the moment you start setting up until the last of the cleanup is done. Go hour by hour. Use the schedule, but include items which are behind-the-scenes. Make sure everyone knows where they are expected to be and when.

Now you are ready to hold your convention. Good luck! Once it is over, don't forget to capture all the lessons learned. Have a final staff meeting and get everyone's input. Write down everything that went well and how you achieved that, as well as what went wrong along with how to avoid it in the future. This will be helpful to you when planning the second year, but it will be a lifesaver if you hand the job over to someone else.

Conclusion

Running a convention is a lot of work. You're going to donate plenty of afternoons and weekends to organizing your event. There are going to be plenty of misunderstandings, hurt feelings, personality conflicts, mistakes, and duplicated work. By the time the convention closes its doors on the last day you may feel like you never want to do this again. However, if you have done a good job then it's at this time that the comments and reviews will start to come in. After a week or two, once you see how many people had a great time, and after you read all the reviews from people who can't wait for next year, you'll probably change your mind. I get that "never again" feeling every time, but two weeks later, I'm planning how we can do even better the next time. While it takes a lot of time and effort to run a convention, it's also a tremendously rewarding experience.

Hopefully, the advice contained in this book will help you to avoid some of the mistakes I, and other first time convention organizers, have made. It can be used like a checklist, but it can't cover every situation. You have to be flexible and embrace change. Have a solid plan, but recognize that the first casualty of war is usually the plan. The ability to think on your feet and improvise is essential.

A great way to find the holes in your plan is to hold a mini-convention. Get with a library or other location that would be willing to let you host a mini con for free, or at least on the cheap. You probably won't be allowed to have vendors, and you definitely won't have the budget for big-name celebrity guests, but you can still practice those skills. Get a local artist or author to serve as your guest of honor. Let local clubs set up fan tables to advertise and recruit. Get volunteers to host panels and contests. Set up a ticketing service, but make the tickets free. This lets every member of your staff practice their job before the big event.

I wish you the best of luck running your convention, and who knows, maybe someday I'll have a table or a panel at your con!

www.ingramcontent.com/pod-product-compliance
Lightning Source LLC
Chambersburg PA
CBHW061029050726
47592CB00004B/1387